Goal Getting with Balance

by

S. PAUL MOEHRING

Goodyear, AZ

Get Squared – Goal Getting with Balance

ISBN: 978-1-7354690-7-2 Hardcover
ISBN: 978-1-7354690-6-5 Paperback
ISBN: 978-1-7354690-5-8 Kindle

Library of Congress: 2020916834

First Published in the USA in 2020

Publisher: Spotlight Publishing™ https://spotlightpublishing.pro
Book Cover: S. Paul Moehring
Editor: Nina Durfee http://NinaDurfee.com – Say It Write
Formatting: Soumi Goswami

For information contact:
S. Paul Moehring
www.SPaulMoehring.com

Goal Getting with Balance

by

S. PAUL MOEHRING

Table of Contents

I dedicate this book to my family for all their encouragement and support.

Foreword

Sit back, buckle up, and enjoy the ride! This book is a quick, easy, and powerful read that will ignite action to generate stunning results. *Get Squared* takes you back to the basics to get solid in what you do best. You will discover the right actions and how to do them for the right results. You will walk away with the tools to set your priorities and align with what matters most. The *Get Squared* process is a simple, step-by-step formula to generate the best plan and greatest outcome in your business and your life.

This simple process delivers big results.

I have never been a fan of this four-letter word: *GOAL*! I never liked the old-fashioned way of setting goals with an attached objective and desired outcome. Goal setting was an exercise, not an experience. The *Get Squared* process is a full-imersion experience. The concept is fundamental and straightforward. Paul's tools help you solidify what you want to accomplish, and then implement it. Have you ever taken the sloppy way out by creating a goal with no plans or backup and then found yourself woefully short of success? This book will take you from the locker room whiteboard into the end-zone, where you'll celebrate your accomplishments.

My favorite is the "Time Management" section, which is a challenge for most. Most of us are managed by time and not the other way around. Paul offers simple methods to organize your activities, tasks, and mentality for daily productivity. I love his "rise-and-shine" concept. Many of us let our day sweep us away, and Paul skillfully puts a stop to that bad habit.

As a professional speaker and event host, I meet a ton of people. I first met Paul in 2019, and we had an instant connection, as if we had known each other since grade school. We are both competitive and driven, inspired, and passionate about helping people perform at their best. In these pages, Paul's commitment to excellence and his desire to leave the world in a better place are forefront. He will inspire you to be a better person and a more intentional human being. Paul's drive and dedication to the success of others is admirable. He fully understands the desire we each have to fulfill our life's mission; he supports that in everything he does, in and out of business.

Dive into this book and do exactly what Paul lays out. The *Get Squared* process is not your everyday goal-setting activity. It has a twist that engages the mind and puts the body into action. Your golden realization will be the importance of attention to and focus on *all* areas of your life. Balance is the key, and this book will guide you and keep you on track and focused on what is critical for your well-being. You need all four wheels to have a smooth ride. Paul reveals the purpose of each wheel and provides the air tank to keep them inflated.

I know that Paul has used, reused, and refined his tools over the past ten years, and this exact process has brought him exponential success in his coaching, sales, and sales management career. I have watched him in action, and it is delightful to behold.

Paul incorporates these principles into his coaching and training business. His dream is for you to apply these processes to ignite your passion and energy. Trust me, Paul can get your energy flowing, and he won't leave you behind. Implement his tools immediately to stay fully determined and organized.

This book is direct and to the point. Paul's knowledge and insight, as well as his candid and straightforward approach, will make you know you, too, can succeed. Follow these principles and take them to heart, and you will experience exponential transformation in your business and in your personal life.

Jane M Powers
Speaker, Sales Trainer, and Best-Selling Author of
Speak with Confidence. Sell with Authority

Chapter 1

What's in a Shape?

"We cannot solve our problems with the same thinking we used when we created them."

– Albert Einstein

It's now today and, therefore, the first day of the rest of your life. The purpose of this book is to help you *Get Squared* so that you can unleash exponential growth in your business and your life. While this is much simpler than Einstein's theory of relativity, it does have a similar component. Instead of MC^2, your solution will be You^2. Any number (greater than 1) squared renders exponential growth, and that's our goal. But please, let me steer clear of math and science; I'm starting to feel that college-final angst rushing over me. I could handle the math classes, but physics definitely wasn't my forte.

Make this book a short, determined read. You'll notice that this book is not especially heavy or dense, and the print isn't microscopic. So, for most of you, we're talking a three-hour read, max. You can finish it easily in the span of a week. So, in keeping with the theme of helping you *Get Squared* with your goals, let's set your first goal to read this book. Here's a quick formula to achieve this easily:

1. Decide what you want to accomplish – *Read this book.*
2. Decide when you want to accomplish it – *Done in seven days.*
3. Decide when and how you will block the time – *At x:xx a.m./p.m., I'll read for 30 minutes.*
4. Define your WHY – *Because I believe the information in this book will help me improve my goal setting, and I'll experience more wins in my business and in my life.*
5. Now, write it down: your goal, the completion time, the time-blocking plan, and your WHY. I'll talk in a later chapter about what to do once you have read the book.
6. This step seems obvious, but *follow through and execute on your plan.* You'll see later that this is the most frequently missed step.

Congratulations! You just set a goal. And if you've heard of S.M.A.R.T. goals, you know that this goal qualifies.

S – Specific

M – Measurable

A – Attainable

R – Realistic

T – Time-based

You're off and running in your new life, so let's move on. Wait a minute, did you read that correctly? *You're off and running in your new life?* That's a bold statement following the simple goal of reading this book, isn't it? Well, not really. If you're like most people, you don't set goals on a regular basis. If you're like most people who set goals, you don't reach them consistently. So, when you apply the wisdom in this book to change your approach to setting goals and you start achieving those goals, you will literally change your life!

What's in a shape? The title *"Get Squared"* serves a dual purpose. First is the exponential growth component that you'll unleash once you've built this process into your life. The other purpose of the title refers to starting with a square mindset. Keep in mind that the concept of *Getting Squared* isn't reserved for you and your goals. *Getting Squared* is fundamental and a sound thought process in a lot of different arenas.

Let's take sports as an example. Since I'm a golf enthusiast, I'll start there. Anytime I take a lesson from a golf pro, they tell me that my setup needs adjustment. They say, "We've got to get your alignment squared up to the target line," or, "You need to do a better job of squaring up the club face at impact." This concept is so critical in golf that getting it right produces a better result immediately.

Another sport – let's take football. The majority of players on the field are squared up prior to the snap of the ball. Offensive linemen square up to their defensive opponent, so they can better protect the running backs or the quarterback. And the quarterback lines up under center, so he can see the entire field and properly get the snap: "Blue 16, red 44, set hut!" Sorry, I love football, especially the Vikings and the Cardinals. But I digress.

Let's look at something other than sports. How about architecture? Where are you right now as you read this? Chances are you are within walls, a floor, and a ceiling. If you're outside, there's probably a building in sight, complete with walls, floors, and ceilings. These walls, floors, and ceilings are all squared up for structural safety and functionality.

One more example (then I promise I'll move on): let's say you owe a contractor for some work on your home. You meet with that person to take care of payment and get all squared up.

What do any of these examples have to do with the concept of *Getting Squared* with your goals? I'll get more detailed in Chapter 4, but you'll be using squares to build a solid foundation for your goals. The fail rate for people setting goals is nearly insurmountable, with only 4% of the population successfully achieving their goals. The purpose of this book is to improve that percentage and make reaching goals more predictably consistent. If you change the way you look at and think about your goals, you will start the kind of momentum that makes great things happen in your life. Yes, it is a life changer. You'll find out very quickly that you, too, can make this work. You'll start it all with some foundationally sound squares. Once your squares are in place, you can build as far out and as far up as you desire. It all starts with a square and solid foundation.

A quick revisit of the goal that you set to finish this book: if you read two chapters per day, you'll be done in less than a week. Read on, *Goal Setter* – don't stop now!

Chapter 2

Our Need to Succeed

"Some people want it to happen, some wish it would happen, others make it happen."

– Michael Jordan

There are 9.6 million Google search results for the words "why we need to win" in quotation marks. Why is winning so important? Society pressures us to win; sports pressure us to win; and we, as humans, love to win. It is intertwined with our DNA. Sure, some of us try to suppress our competitive nature and foster more of a *winning or losing isn't important* mindset, but we really do like to win. Think about it; in sports, does the phrase "fair weather fan" mean anything to you? It obviously refers to those less-than-die-hard fans who show up or watch games when the home team is on a roll and winning. We pay more attention when our team is winning, and when the team we are rooting for wins, we win too!

Here's what's cool: when we win, serotonin is released into our system. It's like a shot of sunshine or listening to your favorite song or band. Bottom line, it makes us feel good. When we start stringing wins together, we feel great. We wake up in the morning raring to go and hit the field of play, whatever that field looks like for us.

See how this can affect your life as a whole? Relationships improve, you are more fun to be around, you feel great, and you are building a winning streak. When you start stacking wins together, you feel like, act like, and develop the confidence of a winner. In your favorite sport, do you ever notice how teams or individuals who are on a winning streak seem to have all the luck? Things just go their way, don't they? Is it because the referees are on their side? Is it because they get special considerations? No. It's because they are on a roll, and they expect to win. Their confidence has skyrocketed, and they've become accustomed to winning, so they intend to continue.

This type of dominance takes its toll on the competition, as well. The opposition sees how good the hot team is, and they struggle in their execution, partly due to the belief that the dominant team will find a way to win. The first time I became aware of this was when I watched the Lakers in the "showtime" era back in the day with Magic, Kareem, Worthy, Scott, and Cooper. Oh, and who can forget Rambus? Their coach, Pat Riley, knew that if their team was down by ten points or less going into the fourth quarter, he'd chalk it up as a win. They were so dominant – and the competitors knew – that come the fourth quarter, look out! It becomes a self-fulfilling prophecy for winners to keep on winning.

Every sport has periods when a winning team is on such a roll that they seem unstoppable. If they continue playing well over multiple years, they might even enter the realm of forever greatness – being recognized as a dynasty. UCLA men's basketball from 1964 to 1975 is said to be the greatest sports dynasty of all time. John Wooden coached his Bruins to ten national championships in eleven years. There had never been a streak like it, and there may never be one like it again. How about the UConn Huskies women's basketball team? They have been a dominant force in NCAA Division 1 play since their first national championship in 1995. Most impressively, they won four championships in a row, and they hold the two longest winning streaks in men's or women's basketball at 90 and 111 consecutive games won.

In individual sports, consider Tiger Woods. Fourteen Major championships and 82 PGA wins have him four behind only Jack Nicklaus for Majors and tied with Sam Sneed for total wins. When Tiger was in his prime, he was tough to beat. He intimidated his competitors with his mental toughness and his ability to hit the right shot when he needed it the most. When competitors crumbled under the pressure of the final nine holes of a championship, Tiger thrived. It was like he was saying to the pressure, "Bring it on." It was amazing to watch.

You get the point that we want to win and then use our wins to fuel confidence and winning streaks. With all of that, we feel the effects of serotonin in our system, and our confidence soars. It was Vince Lombardi, one of the NFL's all-time greatest coaches, who made this phrase popular: "Winning isn't everything, it's the only thing." Let's face it, when you're ready for the opening kickoff in the Super Bowl, it's a benefit to have a positive attitude and keep your eyes focused on the win.

We can leave the literal sense of that statement on the football field. For us in our corporate or entrepreneurial world, winning produces more wins and wins produce positive energy and an undefeatable attitude. You will not fall to the canvas after taking that first punch. You will get up over and over again to face trials, tribulations, and rejection because you know that you'll eventually win. That is what this book intends to accomplish for you. Let's get you winning on a regular basis because that will change your life and deliver the exponential growth you desire.

Remember our "fair-weather fan"? Well really, who could blame him or her? They turn on the TV or head to the stadium only to see their team get beat into the turf. And they think to themselves, why am I putting myself through this? Isn't this supposed to be entertaining for me? Don't I deserve to do something fun with my spare time? All great questions. Fair-weather fans either "desert" their team when the team needs them most, or they avoid an event that is sure to make them feel worse instead of giving them the boost they want. Thank you, serotonin; you ROCK!

Chapter 3

That 4-Letter Word

"It must be borne in mind that the tragedy of life doesn't lie in not reaching your goal. The tragedy lies in having no goal to reach."

– Benjamin Mays

I had a great idea for a speaking engagement that I thought would be interesting to watch play out. When I talk about four-letter words, most people think about profanities. That, of course, is not what I'm talking about, but you'll get the point shortly. At a specific point in my presentation, I would carefully pick a member of the audience and ask them, "What's your favorite four-letter word?" Now if I had found a minister in the audience, I would have probably been safe; my second-best choice would be a quiet, shy type, definitely a lady, and someone I thought would give the correct response. And what would have been the correct response? Well, the way I saw it playing out is the audience would laugh, the lady would be uncomfortable to even speak into the microphone (let alone cuss), and her face would turn red. Then I would redirect and get back on track. The plan sounded good prior to the event, and I was impressed with how cleverly it would play out (in my own mind), but it did require picking the right person. So there I was, I had gotten a feel for the group, I had scoped out the lady I would ask, and the time came for me to pose the question.

I asked her what her name was. "Elaine," she answered.

"Hi, Elaine, nice to meet you. I'm Paul. Tell me, Elaine, what's your favorite four-letter word?"

As I handed her the mic, something in this innocent, shy, reserved lady changed. She got a look in her eyes that screamed road rage. She screwed her face into an evil, angry look, and then she very clearly dropped the f-bomb!

I was shocked. The room erupted in gasps and surprised nervous laughter. Once she had spoken, she reverted to the shy, reserved attendee I had assumed her to be. Her face was beet red, and I could tell that she wanted to crawl under the table. Oh, and me? Yeah, I was flush as well. Once I got the group back under control, I was able to continue and transition to the four-letter word I was referring to. I chalked up that brilliant idea as, "Top 10 list of gags never to try during a live presentation." My wife often reminds me that I'm not as funny as I think I am, to which I usually respond, "Laughter is healthy for our bodies, so if I can make myself laugh, that's all that's necessary."

Let's proceed to the four-letter word I intended: *GOAL*. For most people, this word evokes something similar to any number of profane four-letter words. For some, it's even worse. Some people loathe the word and want to have nothing to do with it. Yet studies prove over and over again that properly planned goals can make a dramatic difference in our performance and our productivity. Countless successful people regularly advise others to set goals and build plans for their futures.

If the word *goal* has such a bad reputation, how can we redeem it? How can we clean up its reputation and send it back out there to drive performance and productivity? As you can surely guess, that is in fact, one of the purposes of this book – to improve the reputation of this awesome four-letter word and return it to the level of greatness that it once held.

First, let's talk about the history of the word. Our modern-day entry-level to goal setting is the concept of New Year's resolutions that some 45% of people take a shot at. This type of goal setting came into existence some 4000 years ago in Babylonia. Back then it had a more religious feel. The same could be said for the Christians in the 1700s, who considered the new year as a renewal and made commitments to better themselves in the upcoming year. Today, New Year's resolutions are mainly secular in nature, and they are usually focused on personal betterment. They represent goal setting for beginners, but they rarely work. Of the 45% of people who set resolutions, about 8% are successful. That means that more than 96% of the population either doesn't set goals or they fail at hitting the goals they set. With odds like that, it's no wonder why so few people set goals. Why set yourself up for failure and drain your self-esteem? What are you, a glutton for punishment?

Many of you have been to a casino, and maybe you've tried your luck at the roulette table. If you were to bet your money on red or black, you'd have a 48.6% chance of winning. You'd feel desperate or simply not very smart if you decided to place a significant bet on it. That's at a 48.6% chance to succeed. What about betting on a single number? Sure, you might have a "feeling" or a "hunch" about betting on your lucky number. Maybe in the elevator down from your hotel room the TV is playing NBA's all-time greatest players clips, and you see Magic Johnson drop off a no-look pass to James Worthy, who promptly dunks the ball, and "showtime" rolls over their opponent. (Okay, I loved the Lakers back in the day.) In that short video clip in the elevator, you were conscious about Magic Johnson's #32. You walk into the casino, and as you pass the roulette table, you have a good feeling about betting on 32 red. You drop your chips on the table and wait for the marble to stop on a number. Lo and behold, it stops on black 9! As the croupier pulls your chips into the casino's pile, you think (one can hope), *I'm not doing that again.*

Now, keep in mind that you have a 2.7% chance, or 37-to-1 odds of winning. What's the likelihood you will place that bet again, and again, and again? Unless you're just not very smart, it's not likely. Let's face it, 2.7% on the roulette table or 4% on a New Year's Resolution are not the type of odds that deliver an abundance of hope.

Goals done wrong are big losers, and that's why this four-letter word has built the reputation that it has. But so many good things can come from goal setting. So, make a commitment, right now. You've already set a goal to finish this book, and you're well into Chapter 3 already, so you're well on your way. Give the *Goal* word a clean bill of health and commit to giving it a shot. (From here on out, I'm going to capitalize the word to give it the respect it deserves.) Forgive *Goal* for making you feel like a failure so many times and recognize that this new approach will take you to the upper 70% of successful *Goal* attainment. Can you imagine a casino offering the gambler a 78% chance to win? They'd be out of business in no time. Flat broke, bankrupt, no more shiny lights and cocktail servers, no more all-you-can-eat buffets – you get the picture. Once you start experiencing winning percentages that high or higher, you'll be strutting around like you just won your third Gold Medal in the Summer Olympics. You'll feel unstoppable and eager for your next event.

Like the song says, "All I do is win, win, win, no matter what!" Okay, I'm getting ahead of myself. You've still got some work to do. Keep reading and turning the pages, and this will continue to come together.

At this point, I want to make one more semantic, stylish, yet psychologically significant, adjustment. From this day forward, do not set Goals. *Huh? Are you crazy? What's the use of all of this "up with Goals" and saving the poor word's reputation? Now you say I can't set Goals? What gives?* Alright, calm down. It's semantics and style that we're looking for here. We want a way to rewire our psychological disposition toward the word *Goal.*

No more *Goal*-setting sessions for you. You need to have *Goal-Getting Sessions.* When you set an alarm for the next morning, it doesn't guarantee that you'll get up when it goes off, right? Someone who says *I'm getting up at 6:00 a.m.* is more likely to do so than someone who says *I'm setting my alarm for 6:00 a.m.* It's almost as if they're suggesting that when the alarm goes off, they'll think about whether to get up or hit snooze. So, no more *Goal* setting, only *Goal Getting.* That will predispose you to achieve and succeed. The mind is a complex machine, and sometimes small adjustments make a big difference.

Chapter 4

The Goal Square

"A goal properly set is halfway reached."

– Zig Ziglar

Are you the type of person who has a fixin' problem? You know the fixin' problem – it's where you're fixin' to thinkin' about gettin' 'round to doin' somethin', but you just can't find the time. I s'pose some folks call this procrastination. I've been fixin' to get 'er done. (Okay, okay, I'll stop typing with a southern drawl.)

A multitude of the entrepreneurs and business leaders we coach are benefiting greatly from *Getting Squared*, and this process is a foundational piece of our coaching relationships. Getting Squared is about getting back to the basics. It's about getting your priorities in order, and it's about beginning with the end in mind. When our company takes on a coaching client, we talk early on about the *Get Squared* process and ask them to fill in our *Goal Square* form. You can go to our website at www.spaulmoehring.com/ and get a copy of *The Goal Square* for three easy payments of $19.99. Just kidding – **it's free!** In fact, you can see it on page 23.

I encourage you to go through this process. If you pay attention to nothing you've read so far and all you do is download *The Goal Square* and fill it out, you will still be way ahead. Your time spent will be an investment with handsome returns. You will be amazed at what you discover. Are you getting the feeling that this process works? We have seen so many examples of transformational thinking and lifestyle changes that I can't overemphasize the importance of this form. Download it and use it. When you fill yours out, send me a quick note on what you discovered. I would love to hear about it from your perspective.

(Contact me through our website, www.spaulmoehring.com/).

What does it mean to *Get Squared*? You can see that the form is basic and straightforward. In fact, it is hard to imagine something so simple can have such a transformational impact on someone's life. But something special happens when you go through this process, and it's not easy to explain. You will see what I mean shortly.

The Goal Square consists of four squares that make up a larger square. On the bottom of your *Goal Square*

are the four categories that you will transfer to the four squares on the form. Those four categories are listed in alphabetical order, not by order of importance. You get to decide what's most important to you. As you look at *The Goal Square*, think of the four categories as the four tires on your car. Category #1 is the left front tire, Category #2 is the right front, and the back two tires are Categories #3 and #4. The car analogy plays out this way. Imagine that you are driving on US Route 93 to Las Vegas from Phoenix. A few years ago, before improvements were made, this was one of the most dangerous stretches of road in the country. There were numerous fatalities on that road every year. Imagine that you are driving on the two-lane portion of the road, and you are separated from oncoming traffic by, well, the yellow line. You are driving the speed limit and paying attention, but all of a sudden, your left front tire blows out.

What happens next is unfortunate. The car pulls toward that flat tire, and you find yourself over the center line looking a semi-truck in the grill. It's lights out for you. If the blowout happened to your front right tire, it would have pulled you toward the shoulder. If the shoulder had some loose gravel, you would lose control, be pulled into the ditch, and roll your car three or four times. Again, it is lights out for you.

As you place the four category headings into their positions of importance, your most vital category will be in the upper left quadrant, and the second most vital will be in the upper right. The other two categories are important, too, but not as critical as the first two. If you get a flat rear tire, you'll have to repair it, but it isn't as likely to be fatal. And two full front tires with two flat back tires won't take you to where you want to go. You've got to properly maintain all of your tires.

Now that you've prioritized the categories, fill in some Goals in each of the boxes. What do you want to happen in each of those categories? This process isn't meant to be knocked out in 60 seconds, so sit down, take some time, and contemplate each category. Our coaching clients love what this exercise does for them, and I trust you will love it too.

I remember when I first completed my *Goal Square.* I took it home and showed my wife and asked for some feedback on the goals I had set for our family. She started to cry and said, "This is really a good idea!" Luckily, I hadn't placed Family into Category #4 – just sayin'. Go to www.spaulmoehring.com/ and download *The Goal Square,* and let's take a look.

As an example, let's work with Ben. He's married to Jen and they have two sons, Ben Jr. who's nine, and Josh who just turned seven. Ben works in sales for You Broke We Fix Medical Equipment Company. His key frustration is that he wants to do the best job he can at work in order to provide income and security for his family, but he struggles for balance in his life. His

Goal Square

#1	#2
1	1
2	2
3	3
4	4
5	5
#3	**#4**
1	1
2	2
3	3
4	4
5	5

Business ***Family*** ***Personal*** ***Spiritual***

Name __________________

position requires travel and long hours. Ultimately, he'd like to start his own business, but that seems like a pipe dream for him at this time. In addition, his work and home schedules demand so much time that Ben constantly struggles to find the time to keep himself in shape. He's often pressed for time, so he eats whatever is handy or easy. These wrong foods don't support his health and don't energize him to combat his stressful schedule.

For his *Goal Square*, Ben put Family in position #1. He had never taken the time to work on goals for his family, so it took him a while to get started. But he was committed to the process, and here's how he filled in his goals.

Family Goal Square

#1	Family
1	Listen to the kids daily. Be present
2	Eat as a family 3x per week minimum
3	Plan 2 family getaways per year
4	Date night once per week
5	

Here is the great thing about using this process with your family: participation. Pick a time when you are enjoying a meal together. Open a discussion about *The Goal Square*, the tires on the car, and the importance of the family unit. Then mention that instead of just getting Goals for work, you would like to get some Goals at home, too. It leads to a fun, maybe even spirited conversation. At the end of the exercise, it strengthens your family as a team, and you learn and develop together.

Before you jump into your *Goal Square*, remember: everything is relative to you and your life. Maybe you don't have kids, maybe you can only think of a couple items, maybe you've got writer's block. Just put your heads together, throw out some ideas, and let your vision and imagination take over.

Now – this minute – is a great time to stop, put this book down, and fill out your *Goal Square*. Don't worry about writing five goals in each category. That's not important. But give it some thought and ask yourself what you really want to accomplish in each category. Once you have completed it, jump back into Chapter 5 to learn about the next steps. Good luck, and don't forget to contact me and drop me a note through our website at www.spaulmoehring.com. I'm very curious to find out what you learn, and I love hearing what people discover while using this tool.

Annie's Story

Annie loved the idea of being in business for herself. She was confident with her abilities, experience, and her education, but the doubts still tended to creep in. When she decided to move forward with her business, it was a committed startup, and she vowed to give it her all to make it a success. She loves her clients, and she does her best to provide quality service and take good care of them by offering the right product solutions.

Annie's business was a success, but after fifteen years, she felt something was missing. Her passion, drive, and will to succeed had diminished; she no longer felt the daily motivation required to hit her goals. Annie believed in continuing education and strived to stay on the cutting edge, so that she could continue to grow and thrive. Although she felt like something was missing, she chalked it up to a mild case of burnout that she was hopeful would pass.

A colleague suggested that she seek out a business coach and referred her to us, as he had experienced success using our services. We began to work with Annie. She was nervous during that first visit, not sure how the whole process would work. Being somewhat private, Annie worried about what would be asked of her. She was not sure she even needed a coach; after all, given her fifteen-year track record, she correctly considered her business to be a success.

Once past her initial discomfort, I asked her questions about her business, her conquests, her frustrations, and her vision for the future. I also asked about her life outside of work. It seemed she had a great family life and that she enjoyed outdoor activities whenever possible. She also enjoyed a glass of wine with friends from time to time.

Her frustration in her business was that she felt as though she was spinning her wheels. Her company was not growing the way she wanted, and her employees were not motivated to perform. Because the wins were not stacking up, her business that she had worked so hard to build now felt like a job. Her business owned her, instead of her owing her business. This is a common frustration we hear from business owners. They feel overworked, underpaid, nobody else cares as much as they do, and they can't possibly do anything more, unless they make major sacrifices in other areas of their lives.

Because we see a lot of business owners with similar frustrations, we were confident that we could help Annie. We had her fill out *The Goal Square* and gave her the framework for using the process. Here is what she said after going through the exercise:

"The *Get Squared* process has been an eye-opener for me from the beginning. I have always been a goal setter, but the phrase *Goal-Getter* struck a chord. The idea of getting Goals in each of the four categories on *The Goal Square* was new for me. I took the time to thoroughly organize the categories into my order of priority. Then I listed a few goals that I wanted to get in each category.

"The entire process was thought-provoking, and to do it right took some time. The whole process was motivating, and I find it helpful to revisit *The Goal Square* on a regular basis. Since I wrote down my goals and started working on each area in my life, it was easier and more rewarding to check off the goals as I achieved them. Some goals that I thought would take a few years to achieve have come much more quickly due to having a clear vision of where I want to go. It has been exciting to work towards making them happen instead of just dreaming about them happening. This process has made me more accountable and more motivated. Now, instead of *setting* goals, I'm actually *getting* them, which is really fun." – Annie

Chapter 5

Activity Planning

"Do what you have to do, to do what you want to do."

– Denzel Washington

To reiterate the point from Chapter 3, we are eliminating the phrase "goal setter" and permanently replacing it with "*Goal Getter,*" and we are replacing goal-setting sessions with *Goal-Getting Sessions.* This is one of the small changes that will take you from the 4% success rate on goal accomplishment (which is the average) to the upper 70% success rate that you deserve.

The next step in the process is to take each one of your Goals and build your plans for accomplishment. The *Get Squared System Worksheet* will help you organize these plans. You can download the form from our website at www.spaulmoehring.com. Successful Goal Getting involves the following steps:

- Clarify what you want to accomplish.
- Determine your action steps to get the Goal.
- Decide when you'll get it done.
- Take action and execute.
- Track results and be accountable.

It's one thing to write down what you want to accomplish. That is better than nothing; but to experience true success and to gain the momentum of stacking up wins, you've got to take it to the next level. You have got to be able to say, "I'm going to get me some Goals!" And *go get them.*

Our next step is to use the *Get Squared System Worksheet* to move you closer to getting your Goals.

Get Squared System Worksheet

Complete one worksheet for each goal that you wrote into your *Goal Square.* Now stay the course, because you will appreciate how powerful the end result will be when you have completed these steps. And remember, almost everybody fails at getting their Goals, but you are improving your odds about twentyfold. Do. The. Work. You will not regret it.

GET SQUARED SYSTEM WORKSHEET

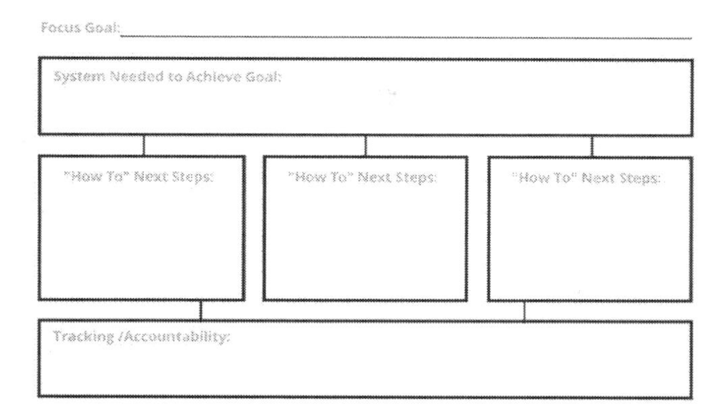

Focus Goal: ______

System Needed to Achieve Goal:

"How To" Next Steps:

"How To" Next Steps:

"How To" Next Steps:

Tracking /Accountability:

Start with your focus *Goal*, then fill in the systems needed to achieve the *Goal*. Continue to the ***"How To" Next Steps*** boxes, and finally, fill in the ***Tracking/Accountability*** section. From a business standpoint, you might think of the last section as your KPIs (Key Performance Indicators). "Winners keep score," and holding yourself accountable on a daily, weekly, and monthly basis will keep you moving toward your goals.

You've heard the phrase *where the rubber meets the road*, and we're there right now with Ben. Let's look at one of his personal Goals. We mentioned that he struggled with eating right and having time to exercise, so

Ben decided that he wanted to lose weight and get back into shape. He was, after all, a 3 sport letterman in high school and played basketball in college before blowing out a knee.

Get Squared System Worksheet

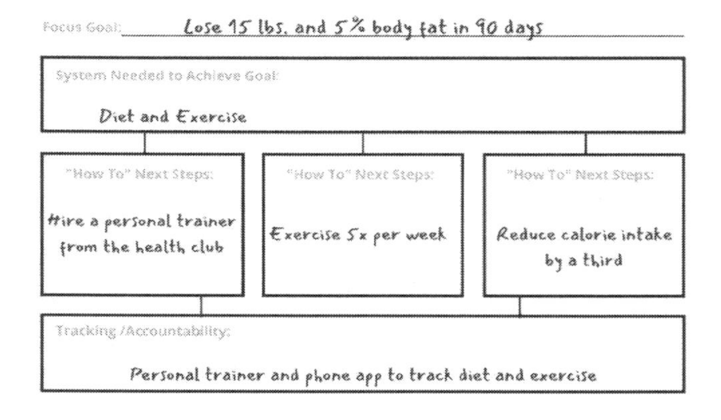
GET SQUARED SYSTEM WORKSHEET

Focus Goal: Lose 15 lbs. and 5% body fat in 90 days

System Needed to Achieve Goal: Diet and Exercise

"How To" Next Steps:	"How To" Next Steps:	"How To" Next Steps:
Hire a personal trainer from the health club	Exercise 5x per week	Reduce calorie intake by a third

Tracking /Accountability: Personal trainer and phone app to track diet and exercise

The clarity of his *Goals* and plans starts to take shape when he takes the 15 pounds and 5% body fat Goal and commits to taking action. I think of this as a reverse engineering process. Start with the end in mind, and then figure out what it will take to get there. Then take action and execute.

Even though this step will take time and dedication, it is impressive how it clarifies your vision and strengthens your resolve. I encourage you to stop reading right here, right now, and mark this page until you've completed your *Get Squared System Worksheet* for each one of your *Goals*. Come back when you're done and be prepared to move forward.

The good news is that once you've completed this *Get Squared* process, you'll be able to methodically and successfully reach new heights and experience transformative success that you've long dreamt about but never thought you'd achieve. And the kicker is that you will achieve that success with balance, which is a huge benefit for you and the people you care about most.

I'll see you next chapter after you've completed this step. And remember, this information is available on our website at www.spaulmoehring.com.

Miranda's Story

Miranda was looking to expand her business when we met with her. She had extensive experience in corporate training and development, but after giving birth to her daughter, even though she loved her job, she chose to be a stay-at-home mom for the early years. When her daughter started school, Miranda wanted back into the workforce. She had dabbled in a home-based business while she was home with her daughter, but she knew that would not provide enough income for her needs.

The corporate training department that she left had been reduced greatly due to economic factors, so Miranda took a customer service position and advanced quickly. That led her back into a training role in an organization. She enjoyed training and supporting new business owners, but she was attracted to the idea of being in business for herself. She liked the flexibility and control that business owners have over their daily and weekly schedules. She also liked the concept that the more you put into the business, the more you will get out of it. Lastly, she had trained a number of new business owners and watched them grow successful businesses, so why not do the same for herself?

Miranda took the leap of faith that many have had to take. It was exciting, daunting, invigorating, and stressful; but at the end of any given week, the positives far outweighed the negatives. She continued to build on her early successes, but after four years she hit a roadblock. Miranda was stressed because she was doing most of the work; but she did not feel that she could afford the costs to hire another person. She was confident that if she could concentrate on her revenue-producing activities, she could make up the additional costs in additional sales. Yet here she was again – needing to take another leap of faith. She was stuck between a rock and a hard place. People commonly face these decisions multiple times in business and in life.

When I met with Miranda, she was seriously contemplating getting out of her business and going a different route – maybe back to a corporate training position, even though that was not her ultimate goal and it made her chest ache to think of closing her business. Last, but certainly not least, the stress that she felt at work carried into her personal life at home.

After our initial visit, we had Miranda work on her *Goal Square* to lay a solid foundation for the future of her business and her personal life. This is her feedback after going through the process:

"What I love about the *Get Squared* concept is that our lives are not made up of just a single component. We live our lives in many different facets, and business goals are not the only goals that we should spend time developing. By using the four quadrants of the *Goal Square,* I can see at a glance the wholeness of my life. I know what's most important to me, and I work on those items first. It is a great reminder, and I keep it handy on my desk so that it's never out of reach or in the bottom of a file drawer. I'm a visual person, so I want to be able to see my goals at a glance. That keeps me on track throughout the month, quarter, and year.

"I was amazed that such a simple tool could help me on such a deep level. Not only have my business results accelerated, but I feel more connected and engaged with my family, as well. In the past, it always felt like an either/or scenario, but not anymore."

Chapter 6

Time and Productivity

"Lost time is never found again."

– Ben Franklin

I've discovered from ancestry.com that I'm related to Ben Franklin's sister. Naturally, I felt compelled to use one of his quotes. In addition to that, Ben Franklin is the godfather of time management. The system that he followed still works today, and I've included a copy here for you. One of the interesting pieces about his system is how straightforward and simple it is. It's not glitzy and glamorous, but if followed consistently, it will make a world of difference.

Ben Franklin Time Management

	Hour	
The morning question, What good shall I do this day?	5	Rise, wash, and address *Powerful Goodness;* contrive day's business and take the resolution of the day; prosecute the present study; and breakfast.
	6	
	7	
	8	Work.
	9	
	10	
	11	
	12	Read or overlook my accounts, and dine.
	1	
	2	Work.
	3	
	4	
	5	
	6	Put things in their places, supper, music, or diversion, or conversation; examination of the day.
	7	
	8	
	9	
Evening question, What good have I done today?	10	Sleep.
	11	
	12	
	1	
	2	
	3	
	4	

You may be wondering, "Why are we sidestepping the *Goal of Getting Squared* for a best-practices discussion on time management?" The reason is quite simple. Good time management is a highly effective modern-day hack, cheat, or shortcut to success. Just so you get it, the reason I describe this as *modern-day* is because the words *hack* and *cheat* often have negative connotations for people from my generation. When I say a *modern-day* hack, cheat, or shortcut to success, you can embrace it and maintain your integrity. It's interesting how our generation gaps produce whole different languages, but that must be how language evolves.

Enough about that, here is the cheat. I know from working with a host of coaching clients that if I can get them to adopt strong time-management habits, they'll automatically increase their productivity and improve their lives. So, if they can do that PLUS *Get Squared* and build more balance, they accelerate the transformation experience. And I can tell you that while it's exhilarating to experience in your own life, it's even more fulfilling to see it happen for someone whom you've guided to achieve it. Why? Because you get the thrill and the rush of energy that comes with the success, but without doing all of the hard work. And even though cheats, hacks, and shortcuts may smooth the road to success, you've still got to put in the work. So, let's get started.

I have compiled a list of similarities that I've learned from studying time-management greats all the way back to Ben Franklin. You, too, can develop your time-management skills and become quite proficient. Sometimes my clients believe that the small changes for time effectiveness are so simple and straightforward that they can't possibly make a difference. That is blatantly wrong.

My Goal is for my clients to adopt and execute these strategies for thirty straight days. If they make it for thirty days, their time management techniques are changed for life, because they have a concrete experience of the positive results of their work. And once you work it into your routine, it's like any other methodically repeated habit. You don't really think about it anymore. It's like riding a bike. (On second thought, I've taken a few spills on my mountain bike over the years, so let's not use that analogy.) It's like brushing your teeth. (There you go.) Now, here is that list of similarities among time-management geniuses:

1. They build systems that they follow almost all the time.
2. They have a consistent rise-and-shine routine that involves about five specific, repeatable activities – everything from workouts to reading.
3. Most have a period of meditation or prayer.
4. As they transition into the workday, they take time to plan out their day.

5. When they start their workday, they are focused, deliberate, and they follow their plan.
6. They work diligently to eliminate distractions.
7. They wrap up their day without leaving a disaster to clean up the next day.
8. They take time to reflect on what they accomplished for the day.

Ben Franklin's routine included a couple of items that were unique. He would declare and work on one of his virtues for the day, and at the end of the day he would ask, "What good have I done today?" Now that's something people are not used to hearing in our society's fast-paced, get-out-there-and-get-yours mindset. Imagine where our world might be if each of us started our day by asking, "What good will I do today?" and ended our day by asking, "What good have I done today?" It's a novel idea and may seem like a pipe dream. But YOU can do it. Not everyone can, but you can do it. So, I strongly encourage you to add that into your daily routine for the next 30 days and see what happens. The impact will surprise you!

One of the tools that my organization uses is a simple to-do list that incorporates a top-ten list. No matter how many electronic apps are at our fingertips, some people just like to write things down. Some research suggests that writing things down helps solidify our purpose and that we are more likely to achieve what we put in writing. I'm a paper person, and I loved the Franklin Planner until I needed a computer-based solution to accommodate sharing my schedule with multiple work associates. When my company developed the tool below, about half of our people used the paper version and the other half used an electronic app instead. What I liked most about it was the Daily Top 10. If you could check off those important items each day, you would make good progress.

How is this different from a to-do list? If I have already planned out my day, why would I need such a form? Great questions. The truth of the matter is that in a fast-paced business environment, things come up. Our team members would start nasty sticky-note habits, and pretty soon they'd have 20 to 30 notes stuck to their desks or attached to their monitors. If you want to shut down one of your team members, give them a 50-item to-do list when you both know they can handle only ten items in a day. It crushes productivity and causes overwhelm. This tool lets team members check off items and avoid the sticky-note desktop decor.

Daily-Weekly Planning with Top 10

DAILY-WEEKLY PLANNING WITH TOP 10

Name: ______________________ Date: ______________________

Priority 1 and Daily Top 10

1. ____________________
2. ____________________
3. ____________________
4. ____________________
5. ____________________
6. ____________________
7. ____________________
8. ____________________
9. ____________________
10. ____________________

Priority 3

1. ____________________
2. ____________________
3. ____________________
4. ____________________
5. ____________________
6. ____________________
7. ____________________
8. ____________________
9. ____________________
10. ____________________

Priority 2

1. ____________________
2. ____________________
3. ____________________
4. ____________________
5. ____________________
6. ____________________
7. ____________________
8. ____________________
9. ____________________
10. ____________________

Priority 4

1. ____________________
2. ____________________
3. ____________________
4. ____________________
5. ____________________
6. ____________________
7. ____________________
8. ____________________
9. ____________________
10. ____________________

Focus Goals

____________________ ____________________
____________________ ____________________
____________________ ____________________

There's something positive and satisfying about checking off what you completed and reflecting back on that at the end of the day.

Access this form on our website at www.spaulmoehring.com.

Let's wrap up time management for now. It is vitally important, and it delivers results. Challenge yourself for the next 30 days, and I guarantee that you will be hooked. We will revisit time management as we move forward and initiate the time-blocking techniques to schedule your days.

Wyatt's Story

Wyatt was an accountant, keeping finances in check and providing a clear picture to CFOs, CEOs, and board members. His work was impeccable, and he felt comfortable in the trusted role of number cruncher behind the scenes. His superiors appreciated his no-nonsense approach and his ability to break the numbers down to a level that others could understand. At times, that felt like a junior-high level, but he loved what he did, and he did it exceptionally well.

For years, Wyatt had a dream, a longing, and a desire to run his own business. He yearned to apply his financial knowledge, business savvy, and strong work ethic to chart his own course. Wyatt met with us, ready to take the leap of faith. He understood that no matter how much he had planned, he would still have to face and overcome some percentage of failure. But Wyatt was ready.

We helped him build a business plan and kick-off his marketing plan, and we watched as he earned his first clients. It was exhilarating to see a child's excitement in his eyes! Wyatt also benefited from three of his family members who shared in his business and its long-term success. His wife has played a permanent role in the business, and her irreplaceable customer service fueled their strong customer retention numbers.

When we introduced the *Get Squared* concept to Wyatt and his team, he put things in priority order. He was already a great planner at work, but this opened up an entirely different perspective. Here's how Wyatt describes it:

"Paul has been my mentor and business coach for over a decade. He is the most authentically positive person I have ever met in my life. When he introduced the *Goal Square* to me, I was struggling through a transition point in my career. The process helped me to focus on the important things in my business and personal life. Working from the goals to the actions put me on the path to successful living and greater personal productivity. The *Goal Square* exercise was a valuable tool for me in so many important ways. It was the impulse to action on my most important priorities. Paul, thank you for introducing me to this life-changing tool."

Chapter 7

Condense and Organize

"Before anything else, preparation is the key to success."

– Alexander Graham Bell

Congratulations! Great work getting this far into the book and, especially, for taking the time to complete your *Goal Square* and your *Get Squared System Worksheets.* You're on the right track, but there are a few more things to consider to accelerate your success.

Most of our clients share a similar thought at this point: they look at their worksheets and start to feel overwhelmed. I agree; it can be overwhelming. But you may have guessed it – I've got just the thing to help with that. Be prepared to be surprised at how well it comes together using the tools available to you here. Long story short, stay the course. You will not regret it.

At this point, you have up to 20 worksheets with detailed activities to get you to your *Goals.* It's time to determine what to do and when to do it. Let's condense and organize your activities so that you can set up your daily and weekly schedule.

Organize your worksheets from Category #1 on *The Goal Square* to Category #4. Once they are in order, transfer the activities onto the *Get Squared Playlist.* This will make scheduling your weeks much more efficient. If it took you an hour or two to schedule each week's activities, you would likely give up. But once you have this *Get Squared Playlist* in order, you'll be scheduling your week with relative ease. Let's take a look at the form.

Get Squared Playlist

GET SQUARED PLAYLIST

Name: ______________________ Date: ______________________

Activity	Category (1-4)	How many times per week?	Specific Day ?	Notes
Listen to kids	#1	7	–	They're not around forever
Eat as a family	#1	3 Minimum	Sun, Wed, Fri	
Date night	#1	1	Sat	
2 Family Trips	#1	–	–	Discuss during family dinner

As you can see, Ben has transferred the activities that he needs to complete on a weekly basis onto his *Get Squared Playlist.*

The items listed relate to his family, since that is his number one category. Of course, you'll fill in the activities from all of your categories. This process is about putting first things first as well, so be sure to start with your categories in order of importance.

Some people like to use color coding in their calendars so they can visually see their high priority activities. Those clients usually color code the activities when they add them to their calendars as well. It's a nice additional reminder about the importance of your activities, but it is not a necessity. We are all built differently, and I'm quite certain that a personality profile would recognize those people who have this ultra-organized trait. Go with what fits you. The more you make this process yours, the more likely you are to use it well into the future.

Once you've completed your playlist, you'll understand the power of having all of your important activities listed in one place. It might still feel overwhelming to look at the list but hang in there; this will reveal an amazing discovery shortly. Stick with me.

It's time to plan your week. Whether you like to plan your next week at the end of the day on Friday, over the weekend on Saturday or Sunday, or first thing in the morning on Monday, you get to choose. The only option that you're not allowed to take is to not plan at all. You're down to the last few steps, and each step builds on the prior, but these last pieces of the puzzle seem to be the most important for our clients. Success or failure hinges on these next items. I have seen some people put together great plans, but when it's time to put those plans into action and execute on them, they completely miss the boat. You don't want to miss the boat – in fact, you want to be the captain of your ship.

Start by taking out your *Get Squared Playlist* and your calendar. It doesn't matter what type of calendar you use. I use Outlook, and it syncs with my phone and Google. Some people prefer paper calendars like the Franklin Planner or one of several other options. What is most important is to schedule and block times to do your activities, and to block those times before the day and week starts. Otherwise, you'll start down the email path, find yourself sidestepping to a social media post, and all of a sudden two hours have passed and you haven't even thought about your important activities. The phrase *letting the tail wag the dog* is apropos here, but you will eliminate that from happening for good if you can start your day by scheduling your important tasks.

Now, there is a big difference between having your *Get Squared Playlist* and having a schedule drawn up. Many time-management experts warn you that to-do lists can cause more damage than good. It is easy to become overwhelmed when all you can do is stare at an insurmountable list of items to complete. The big key here, and the discovery that will blow your socks off, is that once you start planning your day and you commit your actions/activities to your schedule, you will become an efficiency master. You'll be running a well-oiled machine.

This is not rocket science, but there are people who get this and people who do not. The people who get it don't really make a big deal out of it. They act like, "What, doesn't everybody do this? How can they function without it? I wouldn't get anything done without planning out my day!"

That last statement is the amazing discovery that I eluded to earlier. Without using a system like this, it is difficult to get anything done efficiently and effectively. I must admit that I really get excited about people getting to this step. They are so close to experiencing the transformation that they deserve, and they are only a few short steps away. Watching this happen is one of the biggest reasons I enjoy coaching. Positive transformation is *inspiring*.

Okay, let's use Ben as an example again. We took his *Goal Square Playlist* and added the applicable activities to his schedule. For those color-coordinated people out there, we even added the activities with their respective colors from the *Goal Square* categories. Again, not necessary but I must admit, it looks even more organized. A couple of items to notice:

he's scheduled times to handle emails instead of randomly checking all day and letting them interrupt his productivity. He's also scheduled his marketing activities so the day won't get away from him without fulfilling those requirements. Once he wraps up his day, he will have been very productive; and because he was so efficient and effective, he'll go home and happily engage with his family instead of being exhausted and frustrated.

Are you starting to see the benefits? Can you sense that when you use these tools proficiently, transformation is imminent? I hope you're there with me. I ask my clients to think back to a time when their day was this productive, and they get pretty quiet – with good reason. Scheduling your day in advance is a huge boost to your productivity, and if you've only just begun doing that, nothing in the past compares to it.

Here's some more good news. Once you realize that you will be repeating some items on your playlist every day or every week, you can put them in your calendar program as a recurring event and you won't have to spend time scheduling them every day.

To master this planning process, spend the first 15 minutes at the beginning of your work day to do your scheduling, and then be prepared to adjust as necessary when new items come up or completed projects no longer need your time.

Let's take a look at what Ben put together for his Monday.

Sample Calendar – Ben

	MONDAY
5:30 AM	Exercise
6:00 AM	
6:30 AM	Meditation
7:00 AM	
7:30 AM	Daily/Weekly Planning
8:00 AM	Team meeting - review all numbers
8:30 AM	Process email
9:00 AM	
9:30 AM	Follow up by phone - leads list
10:00 AM	
10:30 AM	
11:00 AM	
11:30 AM	Lunch - Salad - Call Jen
12:00 PM	Lunch - Listen to business audio book
12:30 PM	Return phone calls and process email
1:00 PM	
1:30 PM	Prospecting in the field
2:00 PM	
2:30 PM	
3:00 PM	
3:30 PM	Networking group meeting
4:00 PM	
4:30 PM	Return phone calls and process email
5:00 PM	Straighten up desk and look at tomorrow's schedule
5:30 PM	Finish up loose ends
6:00 PM	Dinner with the family
6:30 PM	
7:00 PM	Hang out with Ben and Josh
7:30 PM	
8:00 PM	Catch up with Jen
8:30 PM	Daily devotions
9:00 PM	Push ups, sit ups, and squats

Now, if we were to ask Ben whether this looks like a day that he would label as productive or not, we would get an obvious and affirmative response. How about for you? Is this starting to click for you?

Chapter 8

"D" Is Not for "Discipline"

"Discipline yourself, and others won't need to."

–John Wooden

I'll admit it. I like to mess with words. Earlier in the book I talked about improving the reputation of the word *Goal,* and then I renamed *Goal Setting* to *Goal Getting* and *Goal-Setting sessions* to *Goal-Getting sessions.* Simple semantics, but there are underlying factors that evoke a positive impact versus a negative one.

The title of this chapter is quickly destroyed by John Wooden's words about discipline. In addition, check out the quotes below. By the way, there are more where these came from – thousands.

> *"Discipline is the bridge between goals and accomplishment."*
>
> **—Jim Rohn**

"If you wish to be out front, then act as if you were behind."

— Lao Tzu

"We do today what they won't, so tomorrow we accomplish what they can't."

— Dwayne "The Rock" Johnson

"Winners embrace hard work. They love the discipline of it, the trade-off they're making to win. Losers, on the other hand, see it as a punishment. And that's the difference."

— Lou Holtz

"Discipline is the soul of an army. It makes small numbers formidable; procures success to the weak, and esteem to all."

— George Washington

"A disciplined mind leads to happiness, and an undisciplined mind leads to suffering."

— Dalai Lama

Okay, already? Lots and lots and lots of quotes about self-discipline, so what's my point? The word *discipline* has multiple meanings. Some of those meanings don't sit well with us: disciplinary action, training someone to obey rules, parents or schools disciplining their children. When I'm coaching with clients and we discuss their strengths, they rarely mention self-discipline. Yet, I've got over a thousand quotes touting that single trait as the X-Factor to success.

So what? So, I found another word that resonates better and will lead you to the same success level. That word is… wait for it… *determined*! Determined is *Rocky I*, determined is *Gladiator*, determined is *Hoosiers*. There are truckloads of real-life determination stories in this country and around the world. If you're not focused and determined, you'll come up woefully short of success. So, add *self-disciplined* or *determined* to your list of strengths yesterday and execute that behavior. All of the quotes from these successful people can't be wrong. They will also tell you that self-discipline attracts opportunity and that being determined to win makes for a tough competitor.

How does this apply to the principles and formulas in this book? Getting Squared, planning, taking action and executing, and staying motivated can all be a grind. Performing the right activities day in and day out presents a challenge to most. But if you can take what you have learned, apply it, and build it into your daily and weekly routine, you will enjoy the fruits of your labor. I believe this completely, and I have seen it play out over and over again with people just like you. Normal, everyday people who believe there might be something more for them out there. Also, we've seen successful people use these techniques to take it to the next level. As a bonus, this process will also help you get out of bed in the morning and turn your plans into actions.

As I mentioned in Chapter 5, "Winners keep score." When we work with our coaching clients, we use a reverse engineering process to determine where they should be at any point along the way. We break down *Goals* to monthly, weekly, and sometimes daily Key Performance Indicators, so we can keep a handle on how we are doing toward reaching those *Goals*.

Tracking the numbers closely also gives us the opportunity to celebrate wins. This is a necessity, whether you have a team or you're a solopreneur. Celebrate victories! It is a morale boost to take the time to say thanks or praise a job well done. It also makes the determination or self-discipline more tolerable and worthwhile.

Not sold on celebrating victories? Well, I've always looked at sports as life in fast motion. In sports and in life, we experience wins, losses, setbacks, and lucky or unlucky breaks. Imagine the Minnesota Vikings winning the Super Bowl for the first time in history (could happen) and then the team retreats to the weight room after the game to start preparing for next season. No celebration? That's crazy in the sports world, but sometimes in business, we neglect that piece. That's just wrong so celebrate those wins.

Chapter 9

Leadership and Getting Squared

Life's most persistent and urgent question is,
"What are you doing for others?"

– Martin Luther King Jr.

Leaders face some of the most challenging days, weeks, months, and careers in any organization. They steer the ship, determine which sails to raise and when, ration the food, and make difficult decisions that are not universally accepted. It's enough to make your head spin. But as a leader, that's part of the attraction for you, isn't it? You thrive in difficult situations, you are energized by getting your teams working toward the same common *Goals,* and you are exhilarated by the competition and challenges as you work toward the wins. You'll fight through the agony of defeat on your way to the thrill of victory, and people must never count you out when you are down. Leadership comes with some vital responsibilities, and having your team performing at their very highest level is critical to the success of all concerned.

How can you apply the *Get Squared* concepts to your team to help improve overall performance? First of all, let's face the facts. One of the biggest challenges of being a leader is ensuring your team works together and produces great results, whether you are present or not. That is a sign of strong integrity and commitment by your team. Team members who display a strong sense of pride for that outcome, a healthy level of camaraderie, and the desire to win and succeed make the team an intimidating threat to any competitors.

How does this happen? At its very core, it occurs when the team takes the field expecting to win. And why would they? Because they are accustomed to winning, and that is what they focus on. The organization thrives on the energy produced by the feeling of success and being part of a winning team.

That all sounds great, but where is it born? It starts with great people, people who buy into the culture and the commitment, and people who will follow the leader. Why would these great people follow the leader? Because the leader has earned their confidence and their trust, and they believe that the leader genuinely cares for each and every member of that team. I do not know how many times I've recited to myself as a leader the words of Theodore Roosevelt:

"People don't care how much you know until they know how much you care."

Alright, Paul (you say). What does any of this have to do with the *Get Squared* process? I'm so glad you asked.

Employees in any business believe to some extent that management and leadership always want more. More production, more sales, more marketing, more, more, more. But what if leaders and managers used the *Get Squared* process during an annual or quarterly *Goal-Getting* review? You can strongly encourage your team members to write down and plan for *Goals* in all categories of their lives; but let them know you would like to review their work or business *Goals*. If someone wants to share more, great; but it is not required.

Who wins in a situation like this? Well, assuming that the family is in one of the most important positions on the *Goal Square* like the car example that we used, I would say that the family definitely benefits. After all, the percentage of people who set Goals for their families is, not surprisingly, ridiculously small. Maybe miniscule is a better description. Who else might benefit? Obviously, the individual *Goal-Getter* benefits, because they're being encouraged, not discouraged, to set *Goals* outside of work that help them build a more stable family life, a spiritually grounded life, and magnificent self-care for their personal *Goals*. Every win that they experience, big or small, gives them a shot of serotonin to boost their good feelings. They become more confident and better able to handle setbacks; they are happier, and they work in an organization that sees them not as a number or a production unit, but as a worthy, contributing cohort.

Now you know how the individuals win. But how does the organization win by using the *Get Squared* process? We have helped the people and their families, but what about the mother ship? Here's how it helps the organization.

First, these team members are showing up to a business that cares about them and their overall well-being. That builds trust, which inspires loyalty. The team members are also building up wins in their family and personal lives, and that winning energizes them. When they are called upon to step it up another level to achieve the *Goals* of the team, they are more motivated than in the past. They are also surrounded by team members who are pulling them up, and they are all working well as a group.

Lastly – what we have not yet touched on in this chapter – they have also listed their business *Goals* and started planning their days, so they can be more efficient and effective. Often, when a team member has finished their *Goal Session* with a leader, they bury that form in a drawer, never to be seen again. Why would they do that when their *Goal Square* has the tremendously important personal categories listed on the same page as their work Goals?

Let's face it, leadership is not an exact, repeatable science. But this process has worked over and over again, and it will move your team in the direction you want them to go. And if you're personally using the tool as well and leading by example, they'll respond to that and be more likely to buy into the concept.

To finish up this chapter, think outside of the workbox. This tool is effective for your spouse, your children, your friends, and just about anyone who does not score well in *Goal Getting*. Remember the reaction that my wife had when she first read my *Goal Square* – it brought her to tears! That's another benefit. The word *balance* comes to mind, and balanced growth for anybody in any position is something you don't want to trade away. What have you got to lose? Give those close to you a chance to *Get Squared*. Take what you've learned and help coach them through the process. At the risk of repeating myself, you'll be amazed at the difference that such a simple tool can make.

Remember this important fact: 96% of people either don't set Goals or fail at attaining them. So that four-letter word is not music to their ears. They're going to need some help and support to successfully implement this process. You are equipped to give it a shot; you'll feel great in an entirely different way with them than when you're using it in your own personal situation. Now you are extending your leadership to other areas of your life. And because we're paid in direct correlation to the strength of the services we provide to others, guess what that means for you?

Brandon's Story

Brandon is a sales manager. When we started working with him, he had all but lost his confidence in his leadership abilities. He felt that he was being perceived as background music or white noise to his sales reps, and they were not engaging with him the way that they had in the past. The team's numbers were struggling, and that reflected poorly on Brandon's performance to his higher-ups. He said that he needed to inject his team with some fresh ideas and energy to get them to move again. Once he got the sales momentum to pick up, he was confident that he could keep it going.

I met Brandon at a networking meeting where I had given a *Get Squared* presentation. Something clicked for Brandon when we talked about the impact of the process on building or rebuilding relationships. It made him think of a quote from Zig Ziglar: "You can have everything in life you want, if you will just help other people get what they want." We worked with Brandon to help his team *Get Squared,* and the feedback was eye-opening:

"Nobody has ever asked me to set personal, family, or spiritual goals. It's usually all about *what have you done for me lately?* I have enjoyed involving my family in the process. Thanks for showing this to me."

Another sales rep said, "Brandon, I don't know how you're going to help your numbers by having me work on things outside of work, but good luck. I will admit that going through the process has made me more focused and efficient at work, so maybe that is the key. Either way, like I said, good luck."

In addition, Brandon received several text and email messages thanking him for introducing the *Get Squared* concept. He didn't completely understand what was happening, but he did know that his relationships improved, and his numbers did, too. Again, like Theodore Roosevelt put it: "Nobody cares how much you know, until they know how much you care."

Chapter 10

You CAN and You WILL

"That some achieve great success, is proof to all that others can achieve it as well."

– Abraham Lincoln

If you have made it this far, you're going to achieve the first *Goal* you set in Chapter 1 – you're finishing this book. Maybe you even finished it ahead of schedule. You are a winner, because that, my friend, is a WIN! Small, polite golf clap for you because this is just the beginning.

As I summarize and conclude in this chapter, I'm reminded of the conversations I had with my children when I sent them off to summer camp, to their first sports practice, to their first day at college, or (with my oldest son), prepping him the night before he watched his beautiful bride walk down the aisle. I don't want to miss telling you something important.

Use the strategies in this book, and you'll be a strong, consistent, *Goal Getter.* You'll transform your life! Remember, *Getting Squared* promotes balance and prioritizes what is important to you. Yes, You CAN and You WILL succeed. Throw in the time management and watch yourself get more done in less time. Many people before you have experienced a boatload of success using these concepts, and I'm confident that you will too.

WARNING: Some of you, and you know who you are, skimmed through this book without developing your *Goal Square.* Don't let yourself get away with that. Go to our website, download the tools, and grab the opportunity to experience more in life.

Why might you not have filled out your *Goal Square?* It's obvious and rational – people don't chase after what seems to be predictable failure. You're right to hesitate, but I hope that by now the idea that this can make the difference and accelerate your success is solidifying.

Winning feels good. *Getting Goals* is winning, and when you use these techniques, you'll boost your *Goal* accomplishment level from 4% to over 70%!

Want to release serotonin and brighten your mood? Make your own wins. Once you're on a winning streak, you will want to ride that wave and keep winning.

A bit of wisdom and a few last thoughts to keep in mind:

> *"No plan survives first contact with the enemy. What matters is how quickly the leader is able to adapt."*
>
> **— Tim Harford**

To be prepared for your plans to change, you need fluidity. Your team's ability to adjust and handle audibles is critical, so do not chisel your *Goals* into concrete. Start down the path and realize that change is inevitable. Be ready for anything and poised to adjust and keep moving forward.

Do not be afraid to share what you've learned with someone else. When you teach someone else a concept, you learn it and know it more deeply. I have seen people from all walks of life, age brackets, and socioeconomic classes benefit from *Getting Squared.* Developing these early, strong habits serves the seasoned business person as well as up-and-coming members of younger generations, paving the way for one and all into future success.

You can start this process immediately. You do not have to wait for the next month, next quarter, or next year. Start TODAY and reap the benefits immediately. You deserve the transformative change that *Getting Squared* can deliver in your life and in your business.

Get Squared and enjoy the exponential growth you deserve!

About the Author

Paul Moehring is a Business Coach, Author, Speaker, and Sales Trainer. He lives in the Phoenix area. He's worked in sales, sales management, and business coaching for over 25 years and he is passionate about helping people perform at their very best. After growing up in the Midwest, Paul attended Moorhead State University and was a conference champion pole vaulter and qualified for nationals. After flying to LA for the National Championships and enjoying the weather, he knew that someday he would return to the Southwest.

He graduated with a Business Administration degree with concentrations in management and marketing. After graduation, he accepted a position in retail sales as a management trainee and learned that the ability to build relationships quickly is a vital key to success. Next, he transitioned into the insurance industry where he worked for 27 years. Paul received numerous awards during his insurance career including multiple Presidents Council honors and countless incentive trips.

Knowing that he wanted to pursue a coaching career after insurance, he went through a coaching certification program in 2013 and began coaching entrepreneurs and business leaders. He also built the processes into the training and support that he used for his district sales management. In 2020, Paul began coaching full time and started prioritizing his time so he could finish his book. The *Get Squared* concept that he has used with his clients for years has helped numerous people achieve success in their Goal Getting process. He helps people focus on the most important parts of their lives first.

Paul is available for 1 on 1 and group coaching engagements as well as speaking and sales training opportunities. His energy and presence will keep your group engaged. While mixing in solid fundamentals and principles as well as humor, your event attendees are guaranteed to leave with something they can use immediately.

Work with Paul

I'd love to hear your experience and feedback about the *Get Squared* process. One more time, our website is www.spaulmoehring.com.

To work with us further, we are available for speaking engagements as well as group and 1 on 1 coaching. We offer a free coaching session so that we can assess together the benefits that you may be able to experience by working together. In the meantime, best of luck and continued success. Go *Get them Goals*!

Like what you learned?

We invite you to leave a review!

Made in the USA
Las Vegas, NV
02 November 2022

58631798R00048